Santino's Travel Tales: Riding in Auntie's Car

Author: Lia Tuso

Illustrated by: Nafeesa Arshad

To Auntie (aka Grauntie),
For loving us unconditionally,
Protecting us with all your heart,
And supporting us in every way. We love you always.

Santino packed his bag just right,

He knew his trip would be a delight.

His favorite toys and snacks were near,

He couldn't wait, the time was here.

On the plane, his seat was snug,

Buckled tight with a secure hug.

Mom gave the straps a final check,

Keeping Santino safe on deck.

Santino was excited, ready to go,

He'd soon be flying high, you know!

Off to see Auntie, a special trip,

With his car seat onboard for the plane's long zip.

Up in the air, Santino smiled wide,

With snacks and toys by his side.

He munched and played the whole flight through,

Safe in his seat with so much to do.

When the plane landed, the trip was done,

But Santino's adventure had just begun.

With his car seat in tow, held nice and high,

Santino waved to the big blue sky.

Auntie waited with a big, bright sign,
'Welcome, Santino!' — it was time.
Her smile beamed from ear to ear,
Santino's arrival was finally here.

Welcome
Santino!

They hugged tight and grabbed his gear,
Then off they went, Auntie near.
Together they laughed, hand in hand,
Ready for their fun day planned.

At the car, Auntie paused for a bit,

'It's time for your car seat—we can't forget!'

She gently opened the car door wide,

Preparing to install the seat inside.

When choosing which way Santino's seat should face,

It depends on his age, size and space.

Rear-facing is safest for little kids, don't rush to turn,

Check weight and height, and you'll soon learn!

Auntie, we must read the book,

It shows us where and how to hook!

Santino smiled with a knowing grin,

'Let's follow it step by step to win!

With straps and buckles all in sight,
Auntie knew she had to get it right.
'We'll use the seatbelt or the lower anchors, you see,
But not both — that's what the manufacturer tells me!'

Together they read, line by line,

Checking safety every time.

Santino's finger followed along,

Making sure nothing was wrong.

They found the anchors, clipped them tight,
Auntie made sure it fit just right.
"Click, click," the buckles locked in place,
Santino smiled with a happy face.

Auntie pulled the belt nice and tight,

Santino smiled — everything was right.

She gave a tug, checked side to side,

No more than an inch, secure and wide.

Auntie pulled the harness snug,

Ensuring it gave a perfect hug.

The chest clip placed at armpit height,

To keep Santino safe and right.

They laughed and chatted on the road,

Happy and safe in travel mode.

The road was calm, the sky bright and clear,

And Santino's heart was full of cheer.